SECRETS OF WITHDRAWN
FLIGHT

ANDREW SOLWAY

 Marshall Cavendish
Benchmark
New York

This edition first published in 2011 in the United States of America
by MARSHALL CAVENDISH BENCHMARK
An imprint of Marshall Cavendish Corporation

This publication represents the opinions and views of the author based on Andrew Solway's personal experience, knowledge, and research. The information in this book serves as a general guide only. The author and publisher have used their best efforts in preparing this book and disclaim liability rising directly and indirectly from the use and application of this book.

Planned and produced by Discovery Books Ltd., 2 College Street, Ludlow, Shropshire, SY8 1AN www.discoverybooks.net
Managing editor: Paul Humphrey
Editor: Clare Hibbert
Designer: sprout.uk.com Limited
Illustrator: Stefan Chabluk
Picture researcher: Tom Humphrey

Photo acknowledgments: Corbis: p 19 (Andy Rouse); Creatas: p 5; Getty Images: pp 4 (Fabrice Coffrini/AFP), 7 (Tom Brakefield/Photodisc), 14 (Time Life Pictures/Mansell), 18 (Lionel Bonaventure/AFP); Library of Congress: p 15; NASA: cover and pp 1 Blackbird plane (Dryden Flight Research Center), 29; Shutterstock Images: cover balloon (Vladimir Eremin), cover falcon (EcoPrint), pp 8 (Lobke Peers), 9 (Sylvana Rega), 21 (Ivan Cholakov Gostock-dot-net), 23 (Charles F. McCarthy); Wikimedia: pp 11 (Ra'ike), 12 (DarlArthurS), 24 (NASA), 25 (U.S. Air Force photo/Staff Sgt. Bennie J. Davis III), 26 (NASA), 28 (U.S. Air Force Photo/Lt. Col. Leslie Pratt).

Other Marshall Cavendish Offices:
Marshall Cavendish International (Asia) Private Limited, 1 New Industrial Road, Singapore 536196 • Marshall Cavendish International (Thailand) Co Ltd. 253 Asoke, 12th Flr, Sukhumvit 21 Road, Klongtoey Nua, Wattana, Bangkok 10110, Thailand • Marshall Cavendish (Malaysia) Sdn Bhd, Times Subang, Lot 46, Subang Hi-Tech Industrial Park, Batu Tiga, 40000 Shah Alam, Selangor Darul Ehsan, Malaysia

Marshall Cavendish is a trademark of Times Publishing Limited

The website addresses (URLs) included in this book were valid at the time of going to press. However, because of the nature of the Internet, it is possible that some addresses may have changed, or the sites may have changed or closed down since publication. While the author, packager, and the publisher regret any inconvenience this may cause to the readers, no responsibility for any such changes can be accepted by the author, packager, or publisher.

Every attempt has been made to clear copyright. Should there be any inadvertent omission, please apply to the publisher for rectification.

Library of Congress Cataloging-in-Publication Data

Solway, Andrew.
  Secrets of flight / Andrew Solway.
     p. cm. -- (Science secrets)
  Includes index.
  ISBN 978-1-60870-136-0
  1. Aeronautics--Juvenile literature. 2. Flight--Juvenile literature. I.
  Title.
  TL547.S695 2011
  629.13--dc22
                            2009050539

Printed in China
1 3 6 5 4 2

Contents

Would You Like to Fly?

Imagine being an aircraft pilot. You could pilot an airplane, or the latest stealth fighter. Or perhaps you could fly a microlight. These tiny aircraft have no cockpit, and you fly in the open air. Best of all would be to have your very own wings!

◀ *Swiss inventor Yves Rossy's jet-powered wings are the closest any human has come to flying like a bird.*

In this book you will learn about the science secrets behind flight. What were the first creatures to fly, even before birds? How can a plane fly upside down? What is the fastest plane? What about the slowest? And what will flight be like in the future?

This book answers these and lots of other questions. You can also do some flight investigations of your own. But sadly you won't get to fly like a bird.

EXPERIMENT

SUPPORT FROM THE AIR

We can barely feel the air, so how can it hold up a plane? This experiment shows how air can support weight.

You will need:
- a small, plastic action figure
- tissue paper • scissors
- cotton thread • tape

1. Stand on a chair and drop the toy. Does it fall quickly or slowly?

2. Cut two circles of tissue, 6 inches (15 cm) and 12 in. (30 cm) across. Fold each into quarters, snip off the point, then unfold again. Stick four short lengths of cotton to each circle, one at each crease.

3. Tape the small parachute to your toy. Drop the figure again. Does it fall faster or more slowly?

4. Now try the bigger parachute. How fast does it fall this time?

▼ One advantage of flight is that it allows animals to travel farther and faster. Canada geese migrate thousands of miles each year.

What Keeps Us on the Ground?

Like other land animals, humans can't really get off the ground. We can jump into the air, but we quickly get pulled down again. There is a **force** that is always pulling us toward the Earth. This force is **gravity**. Birds, bats, and insects are pulled down by gravity too, but they have found ways to counteract this pull.

▲ The main forces on an aircraft. As well as gravity and **lift**, there is **thrust** (provided by the engines) and **drag** (air resistance).

How Does Gravity Work?

Gravity is a force that attracts all objects toward each other. The heavier something is (the more **mass** it has), the stronger its gravitational pull. On the Earth's surface, the strongest gravitational pull is from the Earth itself. Its gravity pulls everything toward it.

Large, heavy objects are pulled toward the Earth more strongly than small, light ones. So flying animals and aircraft are designed to be as light as possible. This means they need less force to get off the ground.

SCIENCE SECRETS

COMPOSITES AND ALLOYS

The lighter an aircraft is, the less power it needs to overcome gravity and fly. **Composites** and **alloys** are light, strong materials used in advanced aircraft.

Composites mix materials to get the best of both worlds. Carbon composites combine light, strong carbon with tough plastic **resin**. They make excellent high-performance wings.

Alloys are metal mixtures. One of the lightest alloys, a mixture of aluminium and lithium, is used in the space shuttle.

Superalloys are metal mixtures that work well at high temperatures. Nickel superalloys are used to make jet engine parts.

Overcoming Gravity

When a bird or a plane flies, it has to cancel out the downward force of gravity with an opposite, upward force called lift. Lift is created when air rushes over the wings of a bird or a plane. In level flight, the upward lift exactly matches the downward force of gravity.

▶ *Birds are much lighter than land animals of the same size. A golden eagle weighs only about 8.8 pounds (4 kg).*

What Were the First Fliers?

As far as we know, insects were the first creatures to get off the ground, perhaps 350 million years ago. One theory is that the first airborne insects glided on flaps extending from their bodies.

To glide, the insect must have jumped from a perch. As it fell, air rushing over its wings produced lift, so that the insect could glide.

Insects did not truly fly until they could flap their wings up and down. This allowed them to generate enough lift to take off. Dragonflies were probably the first true fliers, about 300 million years ago.

Go-anywhere Wings

Insect wings are strong, but easily damaged. Some insects have **evolved** ways to protect their wings. Beetles have only one pair of flying wings. The second pair have adapted to become tough wing cases. Thanks to these wing cases, beetles can live underground, in water, and even in wood, and still fly.

▼ *The first dragonflies flew nearly 100 million years before dinosaurs existed.*

A monarch butterfly fueling up on nectar before its marathon migration flight.

Marathon Fliers

Butterflies and moths have large, colorful wings. The colors and patterns on their wings help members of the same species recognize each other.

Butterflies and moths fly slowly, but some of them cover huge distances. Some monarch butterflies migrate over 2,000 miles (3,200 km) each autumn, traveling from Canada to spend the winter in the southern United States and Mexico.

SCIENCE SECRETS

SECRET SENSES

Most insects have two pairs of wings. Flies have just one pair, but they are incredibly acrobatic fliers. They can turn in an instant, hover and even land upside down.

Their secret is two small organs called halteres, which are all that are left of the fly's front wings. The halteres are packed full of **sense organs**. They help the fly to balance, and to sense exactly where it is.

How Are Birds Adapted to Flight?

Insects were the first fliers, but today birds are masters of the air. In addition to wings, birds' bodies have many other adaptations that help them to fly.

Lighten Up

A bird's skeleton is very different from a land animal's. For example, many of the bones in the spine are missing, and others are fused (stuck together). These differences make a bird's skeleton stiffer and lighter.

The actual bones are lighter, too. Instead of being solid all the way through, they contain bubbly spaces, like honeycomb.

A beak is another adaptation that makes birds lighter in the air. It is not as heavy as jaws and teeth, and it needs fewer muscles to make it work.

Fabulous Feathers

Birds are the only animals that have feathers. Feathers provide a very light covering that keeps heat in when it is cold and keeps heat out when it is hot. Feathers also shape a bird's wing and increase its surface area. Without feathers, a bird cannot fly.

Air pockets inside bones

Many vertebrae (back bones) are fused (joined)

Keel

▲ A bird's skeleton. The large keel bone is where the bird's wing muscles attach to the body.

SCIENCE SECRETS

FEATHERS CAME FIRST

Fossils show that the first animals to have feathers were dinosaurs. Most scientists agree that birds evolved from small, feathered dinosaurs. However, they cannot agree on how flight started. Did feathered dinosaurs glide from tree to tree? Or did running, jumping dinosaurs evolve wings to become better hunters?

▲ *The skeleton of* Caudipteryx, *a fossil dinosaur found in China.* Caudipteryx *had no wings, but it had feathers.*

One-way Breathing

When we breathe, we draw air into our lungs, then push it out again. Birds have a more complex breathing system that allows them to get far more **oxygen** out of the air. This allows them to fly at **high altitudes**, where the air is thin and there is less oxygen.

▶ *As well as its lungs, a bird has many* **air sacs**. *These can store extra air and help keep the bird's weight down.*

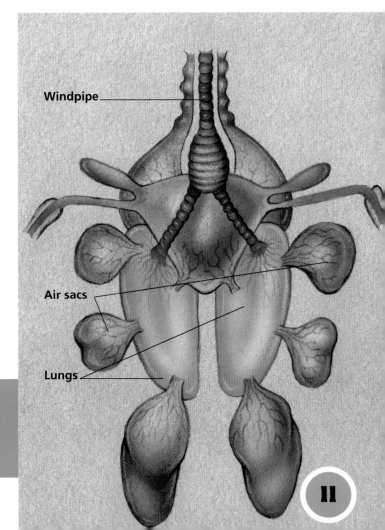

Windpipe

Air sacs

Lungs

How Do Balloons Float?

You can float on your back in water, but you can't float in air. Balloons and airships can, though.

Balloons and airships float because they are lighter than the air around them. To be this light, the balloon has to be filled with a gas that is lighter than air. The gas and the balloon together weigh less than the same amount of air.

▶ *Hot-air balloons fly early in the morning or at dusk, when wind conditions are best for them.*

BOTTLES AND BALLOONS

This experiment looks at how air expands when it is heated.

You will need:
• a small plastic bottle • a balloon
• a bowl

You will also need an adult to help you.

1. Ask the adult to boil some water and pour it into the bowl.

2. Stretch your balloon over the neck of the bottle.

3. Once the water has cooled a little, but is still hot, hold the bottle in it. Be careful not to touch the hot water. The balloon gets bigger because the air in the bottle has warmed and expanded.

4. Take the bottle out of the bowl and pour cold water over it. Watch as the balloon shrinks into the neck of the bottle.

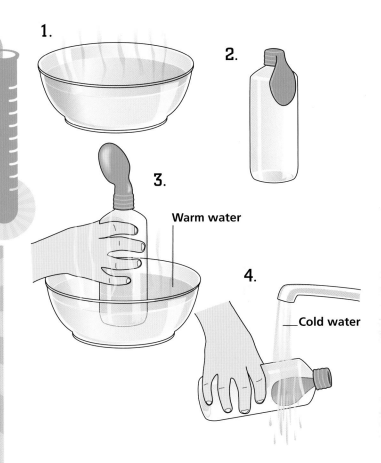

1.
2.
3.
Warm water
4.
Cold water

Types of Balloon

There are three main types of balloon:

• Gas balloons are filled with a very light gas, usually helium. The **gas envelope** (the "bag" that holds the gas) has to be well sealed to make sure that no gas escapes.

• Hot-air balloons rely on the fact that when air is heated, it expands (takes up more space). As it expands, the air becomes less **dense**, and lighter than the surrounding air. The hot-air balloon uses a powerful gas burner to warm the air inside the balloon. The air expands as it warms up, until eventually it is light enough to lift the balloon.

• Airships are streamlined balloons with engines to power them and a **rudder** to steer.

Who Was the First Person to Fly?

The first person ever to fly was probably Chinese. In the fourteenth century, the Italian traveler Marco Polo visited China. He described sailors flying kites that carried people.

Flying on a kite is not "free" flight, because the kite is on a string or rope. The first free flight took place in 1783, in a hot-air balloon built by French brothers Joseph and Étienne Montgolfier. The balloon traveled 5.6 miles (9 km).

▼ *German engineer Otto Lilienthal made more than two thousand glider flights in the 1890s.*

Gliders

The first aircraft into the air were gliders. One of the earliest was designed by British inventor George Cayley, and flew in 1853. Gliders do not have an engine, so they have to be towed, or launched from a height, to get air flowing over their wings. They have long wings to help them get a lot of lift from a slow flow of air. They can also get lift from pockets of warm, rising air, called thermals.

TWISTING THE WINGS

One of the great advances the Wright Brothers made was in controlling the flight of their aircraft. *Flyer I* had a rudder for turning right or left, but its other controls were different from those on a modern aircraft.

At the front were a pair of small wings, called **elevators**, which could be moved to different angles to lift or drop the plane's nose. To control the tilt of the plane, a wing warping control twisted the tips of the wings. When the wing tips were twisted one way, the left wing lifted. When they were twisted the other way, the right wing lifted.

In 1903, the very first powered airplane got off the ground. It was built by American brothers Wilbur and Orville Wright and had a specially designed, extra-light gas engine. On the first flight, the aircraft flew just 121 feet (37 m).

▼ *The Wright Brothers'* Flyer I, *the first plane ever to fly. Its longest flight lasted under a minute.*

How Does a Wing Work?

Wings are the most important parts of any airplane. Without wings, a plane cannot fly. But how do they work?

Producing Lift

When an aircraft begins to move along the ground, air flows over the surface of its wings. The shape of the wings is very important. The top is more curved, while the underside is flatter. The air moves more quickly over the top of the wing, and this produces lower **air pressure** above the wing than below it. The result is a force called lift that pushes the aircraft upward.

However, the wing is also tilted to help produce lift. Any flat surface can produce lift when tilted in the right position, but a wing shape produces more lift and causes less drag.

Taking Control

Once an aircraft is in the air, the pilot needs to be able to control it. Most aircraft have three sets of controls to keep the aircraft level and on course:

1. The tail has a vertical rudder, which can move to steer the aircraft left or right.

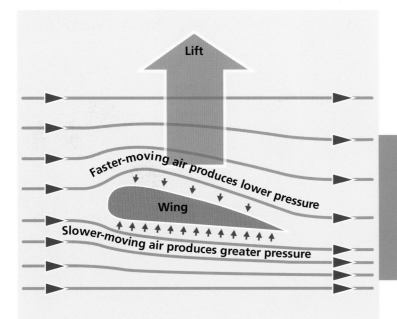

Lift

Faster-moving air produces lower pressure

Wing

Slower-moving air produces greater pressure

◄ *A wing's shape helps it produce lift. Air pressure above the wing is lower than below it, so the overall force is upward.*

2. The horizontal tail surfaces have two flaps called elevators. Tilting the elevators up makes the plane climb; tilting them down makes it dive.

3. Finally, there are two flaps on the wings called **ailerons**. By tilting the ailerons, the pilot can make the plane bank (tilt to the side) or roll.

Aileron

Rudder

Tail

Elevator

▲ The different flaps that control an aircraft's movement.

EXPERIMENT

TESTING LIFT
This experiment shows how air flow creates lift.

You will need:
• sheet of paper • scissors

Cut the paper in half lengthwise. Hold one edge just below your mouth, and blow hard across the top surface. What happens?

Blowing makes the air above the paper move faster, as on the top surface of a wing, so the paper moves upward.

Why Do Planes Have to Fly Quickly?

Staying on the ground takes no **energy**, but staying in the air takes a lot of energy. An aircraft has to constantly move forward to get lift from its wings. The faster it moves, the more lift it gets.

The Best Speed

The lighter an animal or aircraft, the less lift it needs to get off the ground. So a light animal or aircraft can get into the air when traveling slowly. A heavier aircraft needs to travel faster before it has enough lift to get off the ground.

As an animal or aircraft flies faster, the drag caused by air resistance increases. For every flying thing, there is an optimum (best) flying speed, where lift and drag are balanced. The optimum speed depends on weight. A tiny midge has an optimum speed of around 5 miles per hour (8 kph), while the best speed for a large airliner is more than 500 mph (800 kph).

▼ The Airbus A380 is the biggest passenger aircraft in the world. It also has the fastest cruising speed: 560 mph (900 kph).

Taking Off and Landing

Most aircraft need a runway to be able to achieve takeoff. The aircraft has to move quickly down the runway to get air to flow over the wings. When the airflow over the wings is fast enough, there will be enough lift to take off.

When an aircraft lands, it needs to slow down enough so that it "stalls." This means that it goes so slowly that the wings lose lift. Aircraft have flaps called air brakes that tilt up to slow down the aircraft on landing.

► Like an aircraft, a bird brakes to land. It spreads its feathers and extends its legs.

WING SECRETS

The shape of a wing affects how something flies. Long, thin wings give lots of lift, which is good for long-distance fliers. Shorter wings are best for **agility**. Wings that are swept back or even triangular (**delta wings**) are best for **supersonic** planes. These aircraft fly faster than the speed of sound—around 768 mph (1,236 kph).

How Do Aircraft Engines Work

The Wright Brothers' *Flyer*s and other early aircraft were powered by piston engines. These were lighter, more powerful versions of the engines used in cars and trucks.

Many small aircraft still use piston engines. The engine turns a propeller, which pushes air backward as it spins. The backward-moving air drives the aircraft forward.

Most large aircraft are powered by jet engines. Jets produce more forward thrust than piston engines.

How a Jet Works

A jet engine burns **fuel** and compressed air (air sucked in by a **compressor** fan) to produce a jet of hot gases. This jet shoots out of the back of the engine, pushing the aircraft forward.

▼ *Turboprop engines are used for slower planes, such as heavy transport planes and small passenger planes.*

EXPERIMENT

TESTING NEWTON

The secret of how jet engines work is Isaac Newton's third law of motion. This says that every action (force) in one direction produces a reaction, or a force in the opposite direction.

You can see this for yourself by blowing up a balloon, and letting it go. Air shoots out of the balloon, pushing it in the opposite direction.

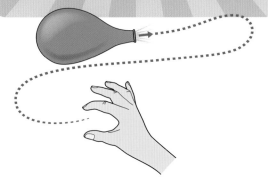

In a **turbojet** engine, some of the hot gases spin a **turbine** (fan blades), which powers the compressor.

Turbofan engines draw in more air than turbojets. Some air burns in the **combustion chamber**. The rest is heated as it flows round the outside of the chamber.

Slower planes use **turboprops**. The jet of hot gases drives a propeller.

▼ *Three kinds of jet engine. Turbojets are noisy and use a lot of fuel. They are rarely used today.*

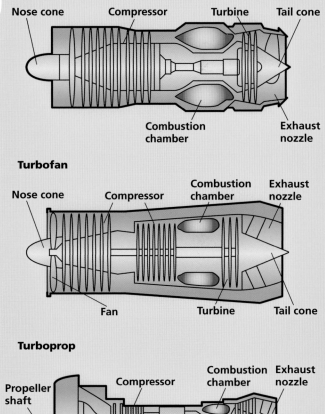

Turbojet

Nose cone   Compressor   Turbine   Tail cone

Combustion chamber   Exhaust nozzle

Turbofan

Nose cone   Compressor   Combustion chamber   Exhaust nozzle

Fan   Turbine   Tail cone

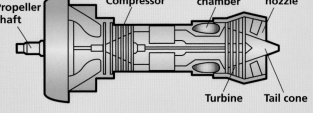

Turboprop

Propeller shaft   Compressor   Combustion chamber   Exhaust nozzle

Turbine   Tail cone

How Does a Helicopter Fly Without Wings?

Birds, insects, bats, and airplanes all have wings. But what about helicopters? Helicopters have **rotor** blades.

Rotor Blades

Instead of wings, a helicopter has several thin blades on a rotor that spins round and round. Some helicopters have two rotors. Each rotor blade is a long, very thin wing.

Vertical Takeoff

A helicopter has a powerful engine that turns the rotor. As the rotor blades spin, air flows over them and generates lift. Because the engine spins the "wings," a helicopter can take off vertically without having to speed down a runway first.

▼ *How a helicopter flies in different directions. To fly left or right, the helicopter rotor tilts. To fly forward or back the whole aircraft tilts.*

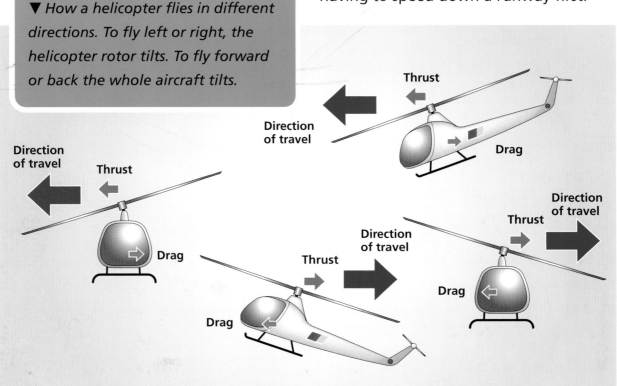

Thrust

Direction of travel

Drag

Direction of travel

Thrust

Drag

Direction of travel

Thrust

Drag

Direction of travel

Thrust

Drag

Piloting a Helicopter

Controlling a helicopter's flight depends on changing the **pitch** (tilt) of the rotor blades. If all the rotor blades are tilted together at a steep angle, they produce more lift than if they are flat. When the blades are pitched steeply, the helicopter rises. When the blades are flat, it sinks.

The pilot can also change the pitch of each rotor blade individually to make the helicopter tilt.

If the rotor tilts forward the helicopter flies forward, and if it tilts backward the helicopter flies backward. If the rotor tilts sideways, the helicopter flies to the left or to the right.

SCIENCE SECRETS

STOPPING THE SPIN

If a helicopter had just one rotor, the whole aircraft would spin around when the rotor started turning. To prevent this from happening, most helicopters have a second, small rotor on a long **tail boom**. The tail rotor produces a turning force in the opposite direction to the main rotor. This stops the helicopter from spinning.

► *The ability of a helicopter to hover makes it ideal for jobs such as this air–sea rescue.*

What Makes a Good Fighter Plane?

Commercial planes are designed to fly long distances as smoothly as possible, using the least amount of fuel. Military aircraft are very different. They need to get to their target fast and be agile, so they can avoid enemies.

Maximum Speed

Military aircraft, especially fighter planes, must move quickly. Many fighters can fly at supersonic speeds. More importantly, they need to be able to accelerate (speed up) rapidly. To do this, fighter engines have an **afterburner**.

The afterburner sprays fuel into the hot jet exhaust. This boosts the engine's power to create extra thrust, but it uses up fuel very quickly.

▶ *An F-22 fighter aircraft using its afterburners for extra acceleration. The exhaust gases glow red-hot.*

THE SECRETS OF STEALTH

Stealth aircraft are designed to be invisible on **radar** so that the enemy cannot track them. The wings and tail are joined together to make one big "flying wing." The rear edges of the wing are jagged, which makes them hard to detect on radar. The engines have special adaptations to hide the hot exhaust jets, and the whole plane is covered in special radar-absorbent paint.

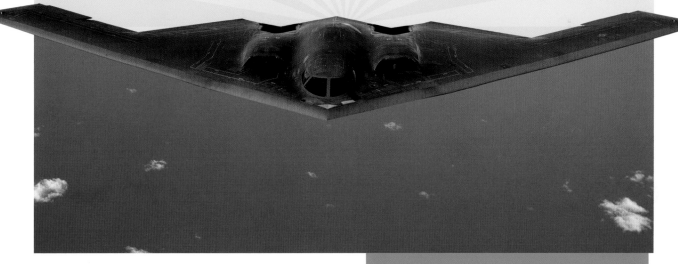

Hard to Fly

Passenger and cargo planes are stable while flying in a straight line, which means that they change direction fairly slowly. A fighter plane needs to be very agile and quick to respond to a sudden change in direction.

Fighter planes are designed to be unstable in flight. The pilot constantly has to correct the plane to keep it flying

▲ *The B-2 stealth bomber. The photo shows its "flying wing" shape and the jagged rear edges of the wings. B-2s entered service in the U.S. Air Force in the late 1990s.*

in a straight line. However, because it is unstable, it is easy to quickly move the plane to one side or the other, or to tilt it into a steep climb or a dive.

How Do Spacecraft Fly?

Spacecraft are designed to fly in space. Instead of jet engines, they use rockets. Rockets are extremely powerful—but that is not the main reason for using them. Quite simply, jet and piston engines do not work properly in space.

Oxygen to Burn

Most engines burn fuel to work. Any kind of burning needs oxygen. Most kinds of engine can get oxygen from the air, but in space there is no air. So rocket engines have to carry their own oxygen supply.

▼ After takeoff, most rockets throw away the large stages or sections that contain the empty fuel tanks.

Fuel Tanks

In the simplest rocket engines there are two "fuel" tanks, one carrying the fuel itself, and the other carrying liquid oxygen. The fuel and oxygen mix in the combustion chamber, where they burn to produce a jet of hot gases. Instead of oxygen, some rockets use a chemical called an oxidizer, which produces oxygen when heated.

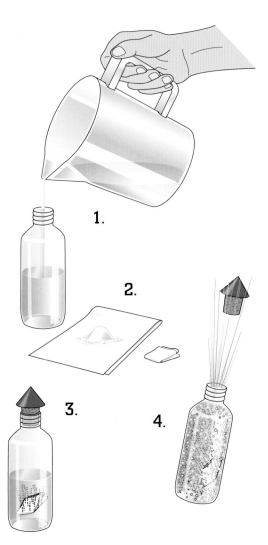

A VINEGAR ROCKET

As in a real rocket, two chemicals mix inside this rocket to form a gas. Carbon dioxide builds up inside the bottle until the pressure pops out the cork.

You will need:
• protective glasses • a small plastic bottle • cork to fit the bottle • 3 tbsp. vinegar • water • 1 tsp. baking soda (not baking powder) • toilet paper • thin cardboard (optional) to make a nose cone for your rocket

Ask an adult to help you, and wear protective glasses. You should do this experiment outside.

1. Put the vinegar in the bottle, then fill the bottle halfway with water.

2. Wrap the baking soda in two layers of toilet paper. Make the packet small enough to fit through the neck of the bottle.

3. Drop the baking soda packet into the bottle and ask your adult helper to quickly add the cork.

4. Place the rocket on the ground and step away. Watch it take off!

What Will Aircraft Be Like in the Future?

Engineers and scientists are always working on improving existing aircraft and developing new ones. The aircraft of the future may use some of these ideas.

Robot Planes

Air forces and navies around the world are already using **UAVs** (unmanned aerial vehicles) for warfare. Robot planes of the future will be faster and designed not to show up on radar. They will be able to turn and maneuver more quickly than manned fighter planes. Tiny robot planes equipped with miniature cameras could make very effective spy planes.

Greener Aircraft

Aircraft of the future will be designed to use less fuel, to reduce **carbon emissions**, and to slow the increase of **global warming**. Scientists and engineers are developing new **biofuels** (fuels made from plants or animal waste) that work in jet engines. Biofuels produce less carbon dioxide than fuels made from oil.

▲ *The Predator B is a robot plane or UAV (unmanned aerial vehicle). It has no pilot on board, but instead is controlled from thousands of miles away.*

SCIENCE SECRETS

NEW WAYS INTO SPACE

Many new ideas are being developed as replacements for rockets. A newer kind of engine used in space is the ion motor. This pushes a stream of ions (electrically charged atoms) out of the back, instead of hot gases.

Future spaceships could also be powered by plasma engines, which heat gases to extremely high temperatures, or by huge "solar sails" that are pushed along by the energy of the light hitting them.

Gravity Power

An exciting idea that could revolutionize flight is the fuel-less, gravity-powered plane. The aircraft has two large tanks full of helium, like an airship, and wings like a passenger plane. At takeoff, the plane rises like a balloon or airship.

At its maximum height of around 10 miles (16 km), the aircraft starts to fly like a glider, gradually sinking downward. As it sinks, wind turbines spin and store energy to power compressed air engines. After gliding for many miles, the helium bags are expanded again, and the plane starts to climb once more.

▲ *An artist's impression of a flying-wing passenger aircraft that could be built by the year 2020.*

Glossary

adaptations Ways that living things change to fit into their environment and way of life.

afterburner A boost given to some jet engines (usually military jets).

agility The ability to perform quick, nimble movements.

aileron A flap on an airplane's wing that is used to make the plane bank (tilt).

air pressure The force of the air pressing down on the Earth. Air pressure varies with height—the higher you go, the less pressure there is, because there is a smaller weight of air pressing down.

air sac An air-filled space in the body of a bird that makes up part of its breathing system.

alloy A material that is a mixture of two or more metals.

biofuel A fuel similar to gas or diesel, which is made from plant material rather than from oil.

carbon emissions The amount of carbon dioxide gas produced by an engine. Carbon dioxide is a major cause of global warming, so it is important to try and reduce an engine's carbon emissions.

combustion chamber The part of a jet or other engine in which the fuel is burned.

composite A material made up of strong, stiff fibers embedded in another material.

compressor A turbine (many-bladed fan) that is used to compress (squash) air or other gas.

delta wing A triangular-shaped wing.

dense Heavy for its size.

drag A force on an aircraft or other vehicle that tends to slow it down. Drag on an aircraft is mainly due to air resistance (air friction).

elevators Two flaps on the tail of an airplane that can be tilted to make the plane climb or dive.

energy The ability to do work or to make changes happen. For example, heat energy powers the engines of a plane, and chemical energy powers a bird's muscles.

evolved To have developed and changed over a long period in response to the environment and to other living things.

force A push or pull.

fossil The remains or the imprint of an animal or plant that lived long ago, usually found in rocks.

fuel A substance that can be burned to release heat energy.

gas envelope The area that holds the gas of an airship or balloon.

global warming A gradual warming of the Earth's climate, taking place over many years.

gravity A force between any two objects that tends to pull them toward each other. The heavier an object, the larger its gravitational pull.

high altitude An area high above the Earth's surface.

lift An upward force on an aircraft, bird, or other flying object.

mass The amount of physical matter that an object contains. On Earth, the mass of an object is the same as its weight.

oxygen A gas that makes up about one-fifth of the air, which animals need to breathe and which is needed for combustion (burning) to happen.

pitch In an aircraft, the angle at which the nose is tilting up or down, which affects the steepness of the climb or descent. In a helicopter, the angle of the rotor blades, which can be adjusted to help control the helicopter's flight.

radar A device that sends out radio waves and picks up the "echoes" produced when the waves bounce back from solid objects. Radar can be used to see objects in the dark, in fog, or out of sight.

resin Natural resins are hardened tree sap. Other resins are plastics with similar properties.

rotor The large spinning blades on top of a helicopter, and the smaller set of spinning blades often found on a helicopter's tail.

rudder On an aircraft, the large flap on the tail that makes the plane turn to the right or left.

sense organ A specialized body structure or organ that picks up information about the world and sends that information to the brain.

stealth aircraft Aircraft that are designed to be very difficult to detect using radar.

supersonic Faster than the speed of sound.

tail boom The long, thin rear section found on many helicopters.

thrust The force driving an aircraft or other vehicle forward.

turbine A kind of many-bladed fan.

turbofan A type of jet engine with a very large fan at the front.

turbojet The earliest kind of jet engine.

turboprop An engine in which jet power is used to drive a propeller.

UAV Short for unmanned aerial vehicle. A "robot plane" that can be controlled from the ground and does not need a pilot.

Further Information

Books
20th Century Inventions: Aircraft by Ole Steen Hansen (Hodder Wayland, 1997)

Birds in Flight: The Art and Science of How Birds Fly by Carrol L. Henderson (Voyageur Press, 2008)

How Machines Work: Aircraft by Ian Graham (Franklin Watts, 2008)

The Simple Science of Flight: From Insects to Jumbo Jets by Henk Tennekes (MIT Press, 2009)

Websites
Aircraft Propeller Introduction
(www.thaitechnics.com/propeller/prop_intro.html)
If you are not sure how an aircraft propeller works, find out here!

Future Flight Design
(http://futureflight.arc.nasa.gov/)
Help design new aircraft and the air transportation system of the future!

Milestones of Flight
(www.nasm.si.edu/exhibitions/gal100/gal100.html)
Find out about the most important developments in flight since the Wright Flyer *took off in 1903.*

Wright *Flyer* Simulation
(www.aiaa.org/content.cfm?pageid=473&vupage=cl_wright)
Try flying the very first aircraft yourself! Even at quarter speed it is very hard to control.

Index